Verses From An Insane Heart...

A book of poems

Maya K.P

BookLeaf Publishing

India | USA | UK

Made with ❤ on the BookLeaf Publishing Platform
www.bookleafpub.in
www.bookleafpub.com

Dedication

To

My Parents- The foundation of my values & my
confidence

My Husband- The source of my inspiration & my love

My sons- The very purpose of my life & my joy

My parents in law- My icons of continual learning

My friends- The reason for my laughter & my cheer

And

My Grandparents- My biggest cheerleaders....

Preface

As a single child, despite my parents' efforts to fill my days with love, I've always felt a sense of loneliness, which has shaped my connection with solitude. Over the years, I've learned to befriend this quiet space, where my crazy thoughts run deep. Some of these poems arise from within, reflecting my thoughts, my inner world, while others are born from the quirky observations from my life. Through these poems, I have tried to explore and understand the wide range of human emotions— from joy to melancholy. This book is truly a collection of verses from an insane heart...

Acknowledgements

From childhood, I enjoyed reading. The world of books awed me with its charm, characters and words. Today, I would like to express my deepest gratitude to all the books that have been my constant companions and the poems that have sparked my imagination right from my childhood. My love for reading and writing has shaped my thinking and perspective, and the power of words continues to inspire me every day.

A special thank you to my husband, whose unwavering encouragement and belief in my writing abilities pushed me to take the leap and try my hand at this. His support has been the very reason that gave me the courage to embark in this journey.

I would also like to acknowledge the help I took from both thesaurus and dictionary for being my supportive tools in helping me find the perfect words to bring my thoughts to life.

This book is a product of all these influences, and I am deeply grateful for them.

4. A journey Inward

Solitude is jubilation
To be alone with self
savouring the essence of your thoughts, being and spirit.

Solitude is rejuvenation
allowing a deep introspection
as you revel in intriguing conversations with your own.

Solitude is recognition
The feel of becoming one with your unmasked spirit
embracing your essence in every inhale.

Solitude is compensation
a rare chance to befriend your inner being
The core that has got clouded
in the wheel of busy mundane.

Solitude is an expedition
stepping into the most fascinating chambers of your
heart

recognising the illusion of emotions and the subtleties of
its expressions.

Solitude is relaxation
A sense of divine quiet that wraps your soul
soothing and nourishing it in its gentle stillness.

Solitude is self - purgation
cleansing you from all thoughts malign,
announcing to you the very purpose of your being!

5. The Riddle of Existence

Life is the biggest paradox,
through tears, we smile,
smiles cement grief,
grief beguiles fear,
fear challenges remorse,
remorse triggers foreboding,
with apprehension we aspire,
aspiration fuels curiosity,
curiosity heralds confusion,
and from confusion blooms clarity.
Life is defined by emotions,
a mix of both known and unknown,
each one propelling the other,
until we sink in its fathomless depths,
worthlessly trying to wriggle out,
least realising that,
Life loses its aura without them!

6. The Voyage

Is this the end?
or just another beginning?
Where am I from & what is my essence?
What is it that I am perpetually searching for?
Where is this leading me to...
helplessly clinging on to a false myth,
Is it a mirage, a deluge or an illusion,
that keeps me waiting, waiting.... and waiting!

7. The Rhythm of Love

Do you know the notes of love?
It's a symmetry of trust, grace and acceptance
It's a pattern of despair, denial and of doubt
It's a matrix of emotions, forgiveness and
acknowledgment.
It's a game of passion, joy, and unending fear.
We strive to master this symmetry
through myriad experiences of our life.
We fall or we rise; we fail, or we win
But at the end of the game, we learn to love....

8. The Myth

When did the journey begin, and where does the path
end?
The moment I was born, I was dead,
My cradle was my grave,
I was born into my shroud,
The real me had vanquished into the deep unknown,
What remains is an illusion,
A non- existing image struggling to make its mark,
in this paradoxically non- existent mortal chaos.
A mirage seeking to unravel the meaning of its
existence...
The voyage had started years back,
The pilgrimage still continues...
I've journeyed far in my quest to create an identity,
I gaze into the mirror and what I envision is the person I
wish to be.
I feel satisfied and reassured at my illusory self,
The image had taken over my true self, the mask has
become my face!

I am lost completely in this facade,
So lost that I fail to recognise myself!

9. A Cigarette's wail...

I was born to be killed!
Ten of us of the same age
packed in a small case
struggling for breath.. we almost forgot light!
Our joys vanquished, our smiles wiped out,
With no sign of freedom, we were waiting to die a
peaceful death.

Miracles at times do happen
An angel came and freed me from the case
Took me in his arms gently paced between his fingers
He showed me light, he gave me new life
My joys found new wings, my hope found new realms..

He loved me and looked at me with care
My fears vanished and I felt like living one full life!
Oh, is this bliss? what men call heaven?
My heart swelt with thoughts unknown.

Minutes passed like ages

He gazed and me took me to his lips
Revitalising me, tantalising me,
I felt overjoyed at the love that was showered....

Alas, even before I could smile in ecstasy
My love burnt me alive....
Death in his arms was life
I was ready to die for him!
He burnt me, smilingly
charring all my body but my heart

Enjoying every puff he took deep,
he played with my heart to ease his mind...
With every puff he took
He reduced my body, mind and soul

All my hopes, prayers and dreams ended
as he threw me down and stamped my small being
mercilessly crushing my heart
with so full of love for him!

One last question spang in my dying heart
Couldn't he have spared at least this part!
Is he selfish or is my love so shallow
That he failed to see my hopes, dreams and desires
and beyond that my heart that held fathomless love for
him!

10. The Revenge

The games of heart are mysterious
Denying what is close, you chase the distant.
Dismissing the familiar, you seek the unknown.
...until it goes too far and haunts you like a bewitching
image
transfixing you with its soothing memories
teaching you the value of your loss!
No running after will help you now
No chase can restore your peace
No tears can cleanse your heart
No prayers will bring them back!
Once lost is lost forever-
moments, love or cheer!
You have chosen this path and now there is no coming
back
You have played this game and now there's no turning
back
For in your busy rut to gather success, you've killed....
Your heart with so many beautiful tiny dreams!

11. An Ode to My Mother

A bundle of paradox
A heap of love
Firm yet tender is my mother.
Without her I am a void
She gave me this world; she gave me my life.
She is my courage and my faith
She is my haven and my solace.
She is my magician, my panacea
She is my wizard, my answer to all
She absorbs my grief and showers me with joy
Taking my troubles, she gives me peace
soothingly she wraps me with her endless love
and I flourish under her shade.
Without her, I am lost—just an empty soul
she defines my existence; without her I fade
I am her part, her youth re lived
I am a gift she has given to me!

12. My Empire

A story I'll tell you
a story of an empire
which I have made my fetters
my routes, and my roots too.

To live in love is effortless
wrapped in the comfort of warmth and gentleness
What is tough is the sail over the murky waters of
hardships
where indifference is difficult to disguise.
To take up the task of staying uneffaced is harder
Holding on without fading away is the hardest of all.

The world outside is a stern task master
judging all your tiny moves-
grading you on its harsh scale of judgement
measuring you against notions of right and wrong,
stamping you with the labels of success or failure.

It's rather easy to live in the world within

where you have no questions, nor answers
It feels secure to cuddle in the cloister of solitude
where you can build your own empire
and curate your rules like an omniscient empress
or soar high in the endless sky of hopes and dreams like
a free bird
or dive deep into the realms of awareness like a mystical
mermaid.
There is no success here, neither is there failure,
there is no right to cheer, neither no wrong to frown
All that we journey through are experiences
guiding us to delve more deeper to this magnificent
empire called Solitude...

13. Life...

Life is gift
So, live it my dear with joy serene
Solve its riddles like an eager child.
Ride it high and low like a passionate racer.
Immerse into its beauty like an adventurous diver
Relish its flavours like an expert chef
Sing along its tunes - merry or melancholic
Dance to its beats- graceful, fast or fierce
Get soaked in its richness like a dew laden grass
Challenge its games with zest and zeal.
Never surrender, no matter the twists and turns.
Don't pause, or falter at its puzzling bends
For, until we die, it is life,
A precious gift meant to be lived!

14. The Cruel Mockery

Truth shows its ugly grin
through all our thick and thin

It mocks us with its menacing smile
shaking our fantasies off miles

Snatching us from the laps of fancy
shaking the roots of existence without any mercy

Turning our beliefs murky and surreal
Teaching the art of compromising with the real

The faiths and values we once mused
Turn confused, or rather misused...

When truth shows its ugly grin
We falter and struggle to win!

15. A Banter

What is a smile? asked a little bird
It's a small curve that wipes all worries, said the little
boy.
What is a tear? asked a little bird
It's a tiny drop that eases a heavy heart, said the little
boy.
What is a frown? asked a little bird
it is a crease that deepens your doubts, said the little boy.
What is laughter? asked a little bird
It is a melody that brings hearts closer, said the little boy.
What is jealousy? asked a little bird
It is a poison that blurs your vision, said the little boy.
What is pride? asked a little bird
It's a tricky tool that can make or break you, said the
little boy.
What is anger? asked a little bird
It is the raging fire that consumes all your joy, said the
little boy.
What is peace? asked a little bird
It is the other word for wisdom, said the little boy.

Then, what is love? asked a little bird
It is life, replied the little boy.
17

16. Master Healer

Love strengthens the soul
We learn to endure grief
Tears don't flow, even at a mighty blow.

Love fortifies the mind
We learn to face the real
Hearts don't shudder, even at the harshest truths.

Love enriches the days
We learn our real purpose
One doesn't dwindle, even at the sharpest pangs.

Love cleanses the heart.
We learn to trust and cherish,
For love is not love if it changes with change.

17. A Teacher's Self Introduction

I am an endless racer
I am a ceaseless pacer
I am an eloquent debater
I am an acronym creator
I am a habitual mimer
I am a walking timer
I am a pun connoisseur
I am life made easier
I am a casual philosopher
I am a novice calligrapher
I am an expert over planner
I am truly a human scanner
I am a daily influencer
I am often a cheer enhancer
I am an unexpected rhymer
I am a perpetual dreamer
I am a spontaneous actor
I am a master director
I am a positive believer

I am a knick- knack retriever
I am a story weaver
I am a solution giver
I am a master imitator
I am a content creator
I am an ardent cheer leader
I am a voracious reader
I am a backstage supporter
I am a smile generator
I am an undying explorer
I am young at heart, forever
All these traits are in my nature
I am who you call - a teacher!

18. My Wait

If I had a choice,
I would embrace death without a second thought.
The giant conqueror who terrifies men
is a solace for people like me!
Do I really live, I ponder...
I exist helplessly- neither dead nor alive!

There were my days—my golden days,
With a loving arrogance, I strode through my home,
A king, a leader, a compassionate family man
I commanded my world, untouchable, like Achilles at his
peak!
But oh! the gods have found my heel!

The sound of the air bed hums like an eerie bird
I lie struggling ; struggling with self, struggling with life
Lying on the bed in my room that's now as white as
death and as pale as hell
I am awakened to the biggest truth of my life- I am
alone!

People who crowded my side seem like aliens now
Their pity shreds me to pieces
Strangers have turned my friends, my unknown kins
With whom I share a bond of agony and pain.

The pain, I can endure, but it's the heart that truly aches.
Fear, love, longing, doubt—show their grin and rip me
apart.
I look at my loved ones, and the pain deepens,
For nothing wounds more than seeing myself as a
burden,
Helplessly retreating into the void of mindlessness.

Once a king, I refuse to yield.
I shield my vulnerability from the world's gaze.
I have mastered the art of existence,
Sharpening my will, step by step.
I have made myself free from thoughts,
I have trained myself to embrace the silence and wait—
peacefully, endlessly.

19. Blessing in disguise

It is hard to be sane
To remain sane is harder
Insanity is perhaps a blessing
A strong shield to fight the ruthless real

Reality shreds you into pieces
It rips dreams apart, slaughters hope,
And carves wounds too deep to heal.
Oh! It pains to be real.

They say that experiences make you learned
But if wisdom comes at the cost of innocence,
Then I despise it.
It does not teach, it devours
gnawing your soul with its deep claws
peeling the warm layers of the heart
The heart so gullible and so full of naive love
Is knowledge gained at the cost of heart, truly worth it?!

Blessed are those who are naive,

who have not trodden the meandering path of cursed
wisdom.
Un known to the busy world, away from the rush,
untouched by jealousy, greed and ceaseless want,
they live a life of innocent bliss!
I wish I was naive too!

20. The Tug Of War

Would someone teach me the art of living
I am a novice, striving to learn
The heart leaps up, the head pulls down
My days oscillate between these two realms
Is the heart too impulsive to trust,
Or the mind too rigid to live by?
I am torn between romance and pedantry
I sway between passion and precision!
If I follow the heart, will it trouble others?
If I follow the head, won't I trouble myself?
I am shattered in the whirlwind of these doubts
Am I the Hamlet of my age!
A coward dwindling between the head and heart!!

The delicate balance of shifting between the two
Is a craft one must perfect.
The acrobatic skill to switch between the two
Is an art that one must master.

Will I ever master this balance, I doubt!

For I falter between the choices...
Like a gymnast striking balance mid air
I still oscillate between emotion and reason!

21. The Catharsis

The storm, the dust and the eerie silence
Teaches me the power of mirth and laughter
The simple blessings of life
That I often took for granted.......

The negative thoughts that blurs mind's lens
Ascertains the power of smile
The instant capsule for positivity
That I often took for granted.....

The busy agile on the task life
Reminds me of childhood days
The easy, cozy, carefree life
That I had taken for granted.....

The long days of solitude
Ironically fill my mind
With a deep longing to reunite
With family, friends, and loved ones

Whom I once took for granted....

The days filled with apprehensions
Heralds the need for faith and trust
My pursuit to fend for calm and strength
Often leads me to the tiny prayer room of my house
Which I often took for granted.....

The new ways of life
The new pages I write
leaves me with lessons in multitude
Urging me to live a life,
Simple and joyous as could be!

22. The Trick

A trick I will tell you
That will ease all your troubles
A simple trick, I'll teach you
That will help you flourish

Learn to laugh... at your success
For they don't last for long
And when you laugh at your success
They lose their power to trap you in their charm

Learn to laugh... at your failures
For they don't last long
And when you laugh at your failures
You deprive them the power to hurt

Now learn to laugh at your self
For that is a skill to master
And when you learn to laugh at your self
You snatch the world the power to laugh at you!

23. The Hidden lessons

The sun whispered
Shine bright but hurt not others with your brightness!
The wind whispered
Flow straight but upset not others with your sudden
gush
The flower whispered
Bloom full but be ready to wither gracefully when time
is due
The bird whispered
Fly high, but forget not the ground to perch
The waves whispered
Rise high but be prepared to recede low
The baby whispered
Observe all but respond only to what deserves
Stars whispered
Shine bright, though you may be one among many
The tree whispered
Grow tall and firm, but be rooted and strong
The rain whispered
Shower on all, but know when to retreat

Every aspect of nature
has lessons invaluable to teach
Pity is the plight of humans
who have no time to halt and take heed!

24. Un Wrap

Unwrap the cover
Unwrap the image
Unwrap the make up
Unwrap the build up
Unwrap the pretentions
Unwrap the expectations
Unwrap the dreams
Unwrap the duties
Unwrap the claims
Unwrap the norms
Unwrap the beliefs
Unwrap the goals
Unwrap the needs
Unwrap the greed
Unwrap the chores
Unwrap the scores
Keep unwrapping the layers
Until you find a tiny glimmer
A small unassuming shine
That is YOU!

25. Life: An Oxymoron in Itself

I have a *simple heart*
That holds *selfless love*
I wear an *honest façade*
And navigate with *clear vision*
Guided by *unbiased opinions,*
My days are filled with *spontaneous routines*
Accompanied by a few *friendly fights,*
They are a collection *of bitter joy.*

Yet, my *altruistic self*
And my collection of *foolish wisdom*
Are undeniably the *only choice*
That help me face the *sweet struggle*
In my quest for a *peaceful life.*

Amidst all these *simple challenges,*
I'm left *clearly confused*
About what life truly is...
But a *constant change*!

26. The Game

Entangled in myriad emotions
Strangled in complex thoughts
Throttled by self-expectations
Chocked in societal pressure
Gagged in the pace for success
Smothered in constant comparison
Baffled in the Dos and Don'ts
Knotted in domestic bonds
We strive endlessly to transform
The otherwise simple life to a complex win- lose game!

27. Memories

Memories are sweet,
cherished, treasured and nourished,
under the warm carpet of heart,
sheltered from threats of time.

Memories are nostalgic,
The illusory image of good that keeps us intact,
we turn our eyes and yearn to live our past,
Taking refuge from the mundane present.

Memories are our friends,
who aid us at the time of dismay,
Gives us comfort and relief,
from isolation, fear and despair.

Memories never leave,
They stay tall and conquer,
till we are enslaved in its grip,
and turn fools in its obsession.

Memories are not truly ours,
for we have no power on them,
We strive to pamper them,
and bring them back to life!

Memories are the past's enchanting wands,
that keeps us hooked in its commands,
intoxicated and entrapped in its chamber,
we relive a life that truly is not now ours.

Memories are like a sorceress,
The pied piper who attracts us all,
We follow her alluring tunes,
hoping to reach the realm of utopia.

28. The Trivial game

Where am I going?
What am I doing?
Is this life really me?
I call it mine
thought on it I have no claim!
Where is the end?
What is the end?
Or does it have any, I doubt!
The game is eternal
The mystery is ever lasting
The journey is never ending

In the morn, I resolve, I promise
At noon, I struggle, still trying
Dawn comes with the same repeating message that
Another day has passed
I retrieve and try again...
Where am I going?
What am I doing?
Is this life really me?

I call it mine...
thought on it I have no claim!

29. Definition of Love

What is love?
Is it a desire?
Is it a need?
Or is the very reason to live?
Is it a smile?
Is it a tear?
Or is it a just another sigh of fear?
Is it anticipation?
Is it denial
Or is an act of complete acceptance?
Is it a bliss?
Is it a paradise?
Or is it what we call as life?

30. What is Life?

What is life? asked God
It is a melody of emotions, said the singer
What is life? asked the God
It's rhapsody of experiences said the dancer
What is life? asked the God
It's a story in progress said the writer
What is life? asked the God
It is lesson to be learnt, said a teacher
What is Life? asked the God
It is a splash of expressions said the painter
What is life? asked the God
It is fathomless thoughts, said the thinker
What is life? asked the God
It is a panorama of drama, said the actor
What is life? asked the god
It is a state for purgation, said the mystic
What is life? asked the God
Life is life- said the child
How should we live? asked the God
As simply as you meant it, replied the child.

At this reply, the God paused and smiled
For all his queries got simply reconciled.

31. Give me a Nod...

From the way we look to how we feel,
From the way we cook to how we feed,
From the way we speak to how we read,
From the way we think to how we act,
From the way we dress to what we wear,
From the way we work to how we repair,
From the way we wish to how we dream,
From the way we play to how we fare,
From the way we drive to how we care,
Every little act hesitates and lingers,
For a nod, a smile or a word of praise ...
Such is the magic of validation,
holding us in its spell!

32. The Trousseau

As I got ready for a new chapter of life
excited at the prospect of playing the role of a wife!
my mother packed a wedding trousseau
a rather humble one...
My father added his share to it
with all his care and fun.
They told me not to open the chest
Until I reached my new nest...

As I embarked on a new journey,
in marriage with my dearest friend,
With loads of hope, awe and wonder,
I opened the box my parents sent.

My mother had packed five real gems
Each one, a shining treasure
For without them I dread to wonder
How my marriage would measure...

The first gem was love, as soft as a dove

My mom said this one will make all my hardships bow!
The second one was care, colourless and bare
My mom said this one will chase away all my scare
The third gem was compromise, without any disguise
My mom said this one will make my life pretty nice.
The fourth gem was cheer, indeed very dear
My mother said this one will remove all my fear
The last gem was the heart, a rare piece of art
My mother said, you'll need this one to play your huge
part!

By the side of my mother's chest,
Lay a tiny one from my dad
I opened to see two sculpting tools
My father sent along, I am glad

The first one was broad and white
Labelled- Confidence in bright
My father told to use that tool
With prudence and wisdom tight
and not let it blend with ego
For together, they can bring much woe.

The second tool was a bigger one
Trust, that weighted a thousand ton
My father said, replace it with none
Without it all work will be undone!

The gifts seemed simple, quiet, and plain,
I wondered if they held much gain.
But through the years, their worth I found,
In joy and love, my life was bound.

Decades passed, yet they still gleam,
Guiding my marriage like a dream.
And when the time comes, I'll pass them on,
For my sons to cherish, when I am gone.

33. I Prefer...

It's better to keep at bay
Photographs that fades memories away.

Of those we love but have gone beyond,
life's reach, and all its bonds.

The mind won't toil neither will it ache
When photos reveal at an instant, the face we search

Better, then, is the effort we spent
to recreate their face in the present.

When I gaze at my mother's photo to view,
The memories feel less and few.

A picture can't bring back to you
Her warmth and love as pure as a dew

When I try to catch her in my mind's lens
My associations with her never ends.

So, I choose to find her in dreams that stay,
In mind's garden where memories play.

No ornate frame, just love's embrace,
A timeless glow in a boundless space.

Call me selfish and it's true,
I build a world where she shines through.

For love, they say, is free and wide,
Yet I keep her close, right by my side.

34. Transformation

Life was truly a mystery,
A puzzle I couldn't unfold.
It wove me into its twisted story,
Till you came and made me bold.

I have found in you a solace
My comfort, a support to lean on
Alone was I, fully bewildered
Unknown from the vicious world

Lonely I had travelled all way
Until my eyes rested on you
Then was the joy of acceptance
Of taking and of being taken!

Life charmingly became a song
Sung in pure deep love
The heart leapt up and hummed in bliss
My doubts and fears, it destroyed..

Life became a poem so bright,
Filled with joy and pure delight.
In every verse, so gently shown,
A stream of love, forever grown.

Life was indeed a mystery
I found it hard to solve
It twined me in its plotted story
Until you came and helped me evolve

9 789369 537181